Copyright © 2018 Tekkan
Artwork Copyright © 2018

All rights reserved.
First Printing, 2018
ISBN 978-1-7324107-1-8

To contact Tekkan please email:
buddhaboy1289@gmail.com

How to Read My Poems

I have married the sonnet to the tanka. I tell a story in the sonnet — using three quatrains, separated by line spaces, and a final couplet. The story builds to a conclusion in the couplet. The tanka is a commentary, or a counterpoint, to the sonnet — the combined poems have two endings.

I don't rhyme my sonnets, because I want freer expression. I want to be direct in my meaning — I want people to clearly understand my meaning. The metaphors are inspired by Shakespeare, and the (aimed-for) precision is in imitation of Japanese style. Using the sonnet with the tanka, I am mixing the sensibility of the Occident and the Orient — which I have done by living in England, Japan, and America.

I don't punctuate much in my poetry. I want the words themselves to do the work. There is logic between words, and the forms provide structure. By not using punctuation I hope to direct readers to carefully attend to each word — to appreciate the graininess of words.

Reading my poems silently, say, on a bus, a train, or an airplane, and reading them aloud, may be different experiences. The way I've written there's not always a pause intended at the end of the line. Hint: *My poems are to be recited not as lines, but as phrases, and a phrase often overflows the break at the end of a line. I pause and take a breath where it seems natural for me to pause. Another person may pause differently than I do.*

Each single poem is a piece of a mosaic, and it is my hope that the collection of poems form an accurate portrait of consciousness.

My daughter, Jocelyn MacDonald, is a wonderful artist. Her art work graces this book.

I am Barry MacDonald. I received the *dharma* name, *Tekkan*, which means, Iron Man, a settled practitioner of great determination.

— *Tekkan*

Everyday Mind II

Only banana

tastes like banana

only a tongue

can taste banana —

I have the joy.

When the wind blows through the bare branches of
The trees on a morning in December
When there's a chill rising from the snow on
The ground when the sky's predominately

Cloudy with scattered stretches of blue there's
A bleakness about the moment as the
Trees epitomize the absence of the
Sun as in stark nakedness they're swaying

In a fierce wind that's not leavened with the
Soothing sound of the leaves and yet there's a
Warmth in my heart and a kind of austere
Beauty about this day that reminds me the

Sun's not really absent life endures and
I discover fortitude in winter.

Suddenly there's a
Pileated woodpecker
on the cottonwood
Striking the tree with its beak —
its scarlet head is lovely.

I became habituated to the
Timing of your episodes with years of
Experience responding to you and
I anticipated your becoming

Angry again your blaming me again
For incidental matters not worth the
Agitation and I was defensive
And I got angry but gradually

With disciplined intention I got good
At balancing my emotions because
I did from the beginning understand
You inherited generations of

Misery from your family and I fought
With myself and became compassionate.

I didn't become
compassionate by hiding
in safe places I
had to suffer myself
and grow with the suffering.

The daughter of the gambler lives today
In the woman who occasionally
Loses control of her emotions who
Disturbs family holidays who harbors

A burning fuse leading to eruption —
And she's not intending to be angry
And she's not aware of her dynamic
Personality as she's reliving

The days when her father ran off with his
Company's money and lost it betting
On horse races as she's repeatedly
Going through the dissolution of her

Family and the unexplainable
Betrayals feeling abandoned again.

I remind myself
I didn't cause the turmoil
can't cure the turmoil
and can't control the turmoil
but compassion is helpful.

Periphery

I couldn't prosper without my circles
Of friends where I take my place as one of
The whole where I go to mix myself with
Others because I need to know how to

Become useful and what role suits me and
Sometimes words flow out as naturally
As breathing and sometimes I catch myself
Measuring who they are and who I am

And I don't seem able to bridge the gap
And I realize they aren't imposing
The sense of separation I'm feeling —
I'm isolating myself because I'm

In a hole of vulnerability —
But now I know the mood will dissipate.

Rediscovering
the role that suits me within
my circle of friends
is child's play when I forget
who I think I am.

I've gotten a lot of mileage out of
Playing the sleepless poet rummaging
For significance and sacrificing
While everyone else is sleeping and I'm

Stubborn and I'll pay the penalty in
Taxes for not having health coverage
I'll stop taking trazodone my magic
Sleeping pills because I refuse to pay

Hundreds of dollars just to consult the
Doctor once just to update prescriptions
So I went to the pharmacy looking
For non-prescription drugs and I talked to

The pharmacist and he impolitely
Asked me so how much coffee do you drink?

Could it be the pot
of coffee I drink each day
lifting me up in
the morning making me buzz
keeping me awake at night?

It's the irascible caw of the crow
Communicating intelligence and
A warning to trespassers it's not a
Joke to linger in its territory

And I know it's not alone a cohort
Of black eyes are watching from the trees and
If I were small enough the menace of
The caw would be terrifying but as

It is I just register the sound and
Think of its sharp beak and remember crows
Stabbing and cutting carcasses of the
Squirrels and rabbits they didn't kill but

Came upon already dead to feast on
While hopping and watching with piercing eyes.

The menace of its
caw the blunt strength of its beak
the enforcement of
territoriality
make the crow formidable.

Of all the things to do she has chosen
To befriend the crows of the neighborhood
By offering chicken or beef to them
And when she emerges from home there is

Recognition and communication
Welcome anticipation in the trees
For her as a small place has become a
Sanctuary from separateness —

Imaginative curiosity
For a bird people ordinarily
Dislike has moved her to offer the crows
The nurturance every creature needs and

There is no telling how simple goodness
May manifest before it's exercised.

Offering friendship
imaginatively so
respectfully so
to the irascible crows
turned the universe a bit.

I seldom consider the beating of
My heart the circulation of my blood
In my arteries and capillaries
As they nourish my toes and finger tips

Because the pulsation within me is
Spontaneous — and every day while I'm
Walking in the bitter cold of winter
I don't often have a clear sky to see

A golden sun rising and even if
I did I might not notice the sun if
I'm pondering politics because the
Sun comes up consistently — but whether

I'm cognizant or not my life depends
On a beating heart and a rising sun.

The circulation
of blood and the burning of
the sun aren't really
identical energies
but they are simpatico.

George says hello with a quivering chirp
As I'm entering the room and he's
Leaning his head on the piano leg
With his back legs sprawling as lazy as

Possible — a portrait of nonchalance —
He's not a kitten anymore and not
A grown-up either and there's not a thing
He does but eat and sleep but he knows my

Habits during the night and leads me to
The necessary room but he ambles
More slowly than I want to go so I
Slow down because I can't get around him

Because George is large and doesn't hurry
And I'm the one who's being disciplined.

George hasn't a mane
isn't on the savanna
doesn't have a pride
but he is brown and does have
a complacent majesty.

I love the morning sunrise transforming
An open sky and casting a shine on
On the snow covered ground with the squirrel
Tracks and the sides and the roofs of the homes

Brilliant because I love to see clearly
Because my thinking is uncluttered and
A natural optimism rises
As if the frictions and complexities

Of yesterday dissolve in the blue sky
And the renewing power of the sun —
But soon my thoughts will assume the burden
Of problems needing solutions and of

Driving emotions and relationships
As I engage with my difficulties.

As if I'm reborn
by the transforming sunrise
as if I'm a child
again liberated from
problems needing solutions.

There's nothing like sub zero wind sculpting
The snow in curvaceous banks and filling
The air with a mist of snow crystals as
Lacerating wind becomes visible

And after a few days the cars become
Caked with the salt on the roads melting the
Ice but also plastering cars about
The tires with a muck of brown ice and

A few minutes in the cold is enough
To zap my glasses and when I enter
The warmth of the house again my lenses
Immediately crust with fog and it

Takes a marshalling of will to leave home
To do the necessary chores of life.

If I let the car
warm up in the driveway for
five minutes it's
not necessary to scrape
the windshield as the ice melts.

I'm ambivalent about a thawing
After the bitter cold and a weighty
Snowfall because it's not as if spring is
Around the corner — we've got three more months

Of winter and all the warming does is
Create an unavoidable world of
Mucky snow on the sidewalks on the roads
And the cars get smeared with salt and crud and

Nothing is beautiful and everything
Sucks and yet the clouds are glowing in the
Morning light as they so gradually
Transform and if I take the time to see

The resplendence here the gossamer there
It's easy to forget inconvenience.

If it were up to
me the temperature would be
twenty degrees from
December to April and
Someone else would shovel snow.

Routine

When meditating in the morning I
Sit on the edge of emptiness as my
Thinking intervenes — when attending a
Circle of sober alcoholics I

Hear unusual stories and muster
As much enthusiasm as I can —
When I arrive at my desk following
The meditation and the circle I

Hunt for inspiration in the sky and
I'm not trying to be happy but I'm
Waiting for an appropriate word to
Apply to an emerging stream of thought

And nothing so far has brought me greater
Satisfaction than morning clarity.

Where I go and what
I do with myself creates
organization
sets the circumstances and
gratitude is natural.

There are moments of awakening that
Aren't altogether enjoyable in
The winter months of Minnesota and
When walking on the asphalt or concrete

After a drizzling that froze into
An almost invisible layer of
Ice we learn to look for a glint of light
Reflecting off the walkway because a

Second's carelessness leads to a quirky
Jerk to discombobulation to an
Impactful connection with a very
Hard surface after which we're completely

Awake realizing penetrating
Insight into the quality of now.

Because I'm spry I
jerk discombobulate but
sometimes I'm able
to catch myself before the
fall discovering balance.

It's not so remarkable — the stainless
Steel the simple utility — it's a
Common implement every household has
So many of but this morning I see

The spoon is composed of sinuous lines
Complementing my fingers and the bowl
Is formed of circles within circles of
Diminishing size perfect for holding

Granola banana blue berries and
Skim milk and I'm not a chimpanzee and
Didn't invent these things myself or pick
The berries or milk the cow — this morning

I recognize all the gifts of breakfast —
Granola banana berries and milk.

Watching the news on
television while eating
breakfast amounts to
mindlessly munching staring —
someone else does my thinking.

Saturday is not an ordinary
Day for me because we assemble in
A chapel with the dawn to meditate
And sharing the quiet enhances the

Quiet communing peacefully deepens
The peace and as thoughts arise we practice
Immobility and as emotions
Emerge we let them go and each journeys

Uniquely and each delves separately but
There's a commonality to human
Consciousness as we derive energy
From each other and together we learn

That agitation is momentary
And cultivated peace is powerful.

I'm not finished yet
not a master of repose
within this moment
and don't have walk-around poise
but I would like to be so.

Circumstances coordinate outcomes
Not always to my satisfaction as
I encountered the invisible ice
While driving down a sloping street and if

Only I hadn't tried to turn I'd have
Been OK but I did and the car slid
As my frantic gestures with the steering
Wheel were operatic but quite useless

So I smacked into a parked car leaving
Minor damage on both vehicles and
Though it's not catastrophic I'd rather
Have nothing to regret but that's life as

Once in a while I fall through a trap door
Of an uncontrollable circumstance.

The spitting freezing
rain is no excuse said the
insurance agent
as the fact remains I lost
control of the vehicle.

As if playing ping-pong with the cashier
At Wal-Mart I ready my paddle and
Serve with a twist my attitude and she
Counters effectively and while driving

I'm playing with position turn signals
And speed as drivers are maneuvering
Beside me reciprocating hitting
The ball in turn and anticipation

Vigilance aggression indifference or
Courtesy arise and usually
I'm not receptive to community
I'm not aware of personality

As we glide by each other attending
To solitary preoccupations.

Without intention
without consideration
spontaneously
I wallop a wicked serve
carelessly imposing me.

Little Me/Big Me

There is part of me that gets pissed off so
Easily when I have to schlep my son
To work because his car needs repairing
But afterwards I'm ashamed of myself

And I hate my volatility and
I realize I am more courteous
With friends and even with strangers than with
My family — it's so easy to lose

My temper and it's impossible to
Erase an outburst — but yet there is a
Part of me emanating from the flame
Of life — the bare awareness — deeper than

Any transitory emotion that
Is carefully watching and abiding.

I can become
quiet enough
to watch emotion
come and go and
be the watcher.

I wasn't pleased when you failed the driving
Test five times because I was sure we'd done
Enough for success — going from around
The block to merging onto the highway

To parallel parking — you were afraid
Of driving in traffic and I was too
Because I wasn't in control but you
Got comfortable enough and every time

You failed a test my frustration grew as
You just couldn't get over nervousness
So much like me at your age but we kept
Trying and the day you passed I was proud

And now you're leaving home for Alaska
Going a long way from home — just like me.

Leaving for Japan
and Galveston Texas too
I said goodbye twice
To my parents and my home —
It's a necessary test.

A word carries a meaning and a string
Of words make a sentence carrying a
More composed meaning making a point that
May be worth remembering and saying

Hippopotamus makes me wonder why
This pell-mell collection of syllables
Is stuck to that creature because the word
Hippopotamus can't be said primly

Or lackadaisily without losing
Dignity and if you're serious when
You say hippopotamus you have to
Use a neutral inflection and also

The cadence should be a bit quicker than
An ordinary word — so be careful.

Usually I
don't have to enunciate
hippopotamus
or also rhinoceros —
But when I do I'm ready.

It's a dull day nearing winter's ending
As the snow's been melting on the roofs and
A shrunken remnant remains as snow on
The ground is crusty and surviving piles

On the sides of the roads are gritty with
Sand and salt and the afternoon thaw and
The overnight freeze has distorted what
Appeared shapely into desolation —

But the sky is clear the temperature
Is mild and in a clearing between trees
A couple of white cranes fly across with
Their long necks pointing their direction and

The stroking of their wings is synchronized
And then they vanish as the sun rises.

Winter drags and
I lapse into
a languor but
it's possible
to be happy.

Every morning I come to my desk and
Look out a window seeing above the
River valley a far horizon in
The sky and on sunny days there's a clear

Demarcation of the blue sky and a
Wide expanse of farm fields but this morning
It's drizzling and there's only a line
Separating the lighter grey of sky

And the darker grey of earth — on some days
Clarity allows me to see distance
On other days my vision is cloudy
But everyday I'm grateful to have a

Window facing east to watch as the sun
Gathers prominence as the night retreats.

Even the cloudy
mornings are miraculous
once I notice how
an overcast sky softly
glows with penetrating light.

The word processing program is open
My fingers are poised over the keyboard
But I'm mesmerized with the white of the
Screen noticing the cursor is blinking

As if the computer were expressing
Impatience so I look at cobwebs in
The corners of the windowsill — at dust
On top of the books on the shelf — and take

Another swig of coffee putting an
Elbow on the desk putting my chin in
The cup of my hand thinking I should be
Inspired by now and then I see a

Pink horizon with an orange disk with
Yellow light spreading and blue sky above.

The cottonwood the
apple tree and the maple
are dark forms without
texture but as the light spreads
the grainy bark emerges.

Screen Saver Daughter

I've been using the pencil drawing you
Did of yourself to welcome me on the
Monitor every morning and there's not
A sharp dividing line anywhere — there's

Shading creating shapeliness rising
Off the screen presenting your cheeks and chin —
And your eyes are black globes reflecting light
And your long hair is resplendent with light

Because you were already skillful as
A teenager and with the simplest
Tools you captured personality and
More than ten years ago within some hours

You drew yourself — which is natural and
Proper — in your perpetual teenage.

Then I start clicking
with my mouse going to my
usual sites on
the web encountering the
depravity of the world.

The jihadists are bombing and burning
And beheading heretics while the North
Koreans are testing missiles — learning
How to aim — while the Russians have shot down

An airliner — and in America
The FBI has figured out how to
Trigger the microphones in cell phones and
In televisions and they can listen

To anyone — and the NSA is
Managing to keep records of every
Phone call Americans make and they are
Also collecting every text message

Americans send and so there is no
Place to hide while I am doing my Zen.

Zen
clarifies
being
focusing
on now.

It was cold again overnight so I
Wore a warm shirt and put my phone in
A pocket for convenience and I was
Crabby because I had to scrape the ice

Off my windshield my nose was running and
I felt a cold coming on and moving
Was difficult and then my phone started
Ringing and I grumbled — who's calling me

Now and I'm not unzipping my coat to
Get to the phone — and then I realized
Because my ringtone is the singing of
A robin — I was wrong — it wasn't the

Phone but a robin I was hearing on
A chilly morning on the verge of spring.

And with a woozy
head a sloppy nose and moving
with difficulty
I felt a little foolish
and a little happier.

There's a glow inside that's not due to the
Caffeine in my coffee not discouraged
By the damp and gloom of an overcast
Morning in April after a night of

Rain and it's not exhilaration or
Excitement and if I weren't alert I
Wouldn't notice and if I hadn't had
Troubles it wouldn't be noticeable —

Like a lamp in the night I'm cheered on a
Gloomy day because somehow I believe
My being is indestructible and
However many mistakes I've made I

Am a flame glimmering in the darkness
And the darkness is inspired with life.

I see persistence
in the roots in the thickness
in the greening of
the grass again in April
as the sun begins to burn.

There is music before dawn as the birds
Have returned and though the grass is crunchy
With frost underfoot the deep freeze will be
Lifting from the earth precipitously

And already there are eagles skimming
Currents of air and soon there'll be swallows
Cutting the air and when I see bees buzz
In summer I will wear as little as

Possible — Imagine seeing the earth
From the vantage of the moon with God's eyes
As it circles the sun and revolves on
Its axis — wouldn't the dawning light be

So much like a wave ceaselessly cresting
With night receding and blue sky surging?

Acquire perspective
indulge imagination
because it's a gift
to be lost in wonderment
and to ponder why we're here.

It's cloudy along the horizon and
Above there's a single cloud that looks like
The strokes of a brush transforming in the
Wind and then a blur of movement becomes

Sparrows alighting in the cottonwood
The maple and the apple tree and as
They fly and vanish I see on every
Branch of every tree buds are emerging —

I can't stay long because there's work to do
And nobody's paying me to loiter
But I linger long enough to take a
Breath and close my eyes and see my lids are

Red with the light and there is the touch
Of sun on my face and wind in my ears.

There is no other
time but now as the
sky is hiding the
stars and I'm busy —
I can loiter.

Crossing a threshold and absorbing light
There's a connection to be imagined
In a baby seeing swirls of color
And hearing startling and soothing sounds

Experiencing taste distinguishing
The warming power of a smiling face
A comforting voice with an embrace — and
As leaves of the trees emerge and absorb

The light as the roots consume nutrients
From a thawing soil the tree will never
Know it's a tree — but when the gnawing of
Hunger comes the baby discovers how

To manipulate others by crying —
Nurturance arises magically.

Before the things of
the world acquire names there's
no distinguishing
within a baby's thinking
between inside and outside.

A brilliant sky with not a whiff of a
Cloud is a break from the difficulties
Of earning money and the discipline
Required of working with people as

It's resplendent and glorious and it's
Filled with sunlight that happens to be blue
As the sky is showering nourishment
On leaves grass and the sparkling river —

And this is the season the earth responds
With uprising grass and a profusion
Of blossoms and whatever business I
Have within doors can wait for a moment

As I close my eyes and enjoy the sun
And my face is absorbed in a warm glow.

Didn't realize
my daughter's graduation
would take away her
dependence status and make
my taxes rocket sky high.

The impetuous chickadee chicks see
The hummingbird hover at its feeder
And suck the nectar with its long beak and
They want to hover at the feeder suck

The nectar too but their beaks are stubby and
Their wings can't hover so they're bewildered
But soon enough they discover unique
Abilities and flit between the trees

Together and sing their chickadee songs
And they find chickadee feeders and the
Chickadees become the chickadees they're
Supposed to be and if they can do that

You'd suppose it'd be easy for me to
Uncover the person I'm supposed to be.

Do I resemble
an eagle a peacock a
flamingo or a
loon a parrot an ostrich
or just a common sparrow?

Thirty years ago it was pouring down
On the cement steps outside my open
Window and I remember the rain on
Concrete as the epitome of cool

And the steady pattering was welcome
As an oasis that summer night in
Kyoto where it's humid and the heat is
Oppressive and I was always sweating —

I was breathing in the moist air and my
Nose was tingling with the water and
Instead of tossing wanting escape I
Was wrapping myself in a blanket for

Warmth and the melody of the rain was
Like a lullaby on the edge of sleep.

The air was heavy
and I was breathing
coolness and tasting
the spattering — the
pattering was soothing.

It's not usually noticeable
With no bearing on my chores today and
Within the context of our furious
Political warfare it's laughable

But a sunrise with a canopy of
Orange and purple clouds inspires thought —
Every soul who's lived has shared this sight and
I couldn't take a single breath without

Its grace as the sun's presence underlies
Our living and within its rotating
Seasons recur the possibilities
Of fruition and ultimate demise —

It's the utter simplicity of light
That it has the power to foster life.

As the sun burns and
gives the earth the day and night
as the foliage grows
and provides breathable air
I have to make my choices.

The eagle sways and drifts in currents of
Air skimming and unconcerned about the
Direction of the wind as it's hunting
And following the movement of fish in

The water as the buffeting of wind and
The adjusting of wings and tail feathers
Comes as naturally as breathing and
If it chose instantaneously it

Would drop and strike with its talons to crush
And tear with a mighty grip and so death
Happens suddenly in the world and as
A symbol for comprehending eyes the

Eagle is a magnificent image —
Everything I know could instantly end.

There's night and day and
spring summer fall and winter
there's youth and aging
and my preoccupations —
just temporarily so.

I love my eyesight but there came a point
When reading became difficult and my
Eyes today often feel tired — imagine
Unlimited vision three hundred and

Sixty degrees from a point that's also
Unlimited that in a whim could go
Anywhere — and imagine seeing from
Here to whatever edge the expanding

Universe has — and then imagine each
Sensation similarly unbounded
By space and time and the constrictions of
A personality suffering the

Vulnerabilities inherent in
In a body destined to disappear.

I can't
Imagine a
Consciousness
Commensurate with
Unbounded sensation.

A Night Out

To do ecstatic poetry it helps
To be in ecstasy I suppose and
I went to a gathering of Rumi
Enthusiasts and with my friends we heard

Music with repetitive lyrics with
Pulsating rhythm and frequently I
Felt in the singers' vibrato both
Sorrow and joy indistinguishable

And the words of the poetry spoke of
Drums and tambourines of stars and moon — of
Dissolving inside and outside and of
Opening the door to visitations

Of all emotions without favorites
And most of all I heard about the friend.

Dancing one circle
Inside another holding
Hands and rotating
In opposite directions
we greeted ourselves in turn.

Perhaps I've been a little careless in
Raising my kids and perhaps I was too
Self-absorbed to give much thought to molding
Their personalities as I let them

Grow without weeding but — like a bolt of
Lighting — I was hit with a memory
Of the frown my father imposed on me
Because the frown communicated such

Embarrassment and disapproval and
I felt shame — and anger — that he would be
So aggressive — then shame and dependence
Began to percolate with rebellion —

One generation after another
We do perpetuate imperfections.

We muddle through with
dispositions attitudes
personality
imposing on each other
without recognizing how.

As one of billions I don't amount to
Much but as a dad I'm a colossus
To a son and daughter from the moment
When I held them after they were born to

Their graduation from college into
Today I've fretted about their prospects
I've witnessed the procession of friends the
Dissolution of friendships — I've been there

When they became secretive I became
Tiresome and disappointing to them
When they resisted my guidance and deeds
Because I didn't know how to deflect

The silence and just as they're becoming
Confident and productive they're leaving.

There are days in the
year each of us celebrate
that acquire more
significance as we age
and for me it's father's day.

Just wisps of clouds are drifting along and
Could any image be more opposed to
Concentrating on the second hand as
It ticks across the numbers of a watch?

And I may choose either method to mark
The passage of time and whether I look
Up or down depends at the moment on
How much pressure I allow myself to

Feel — the numbers represent the need for
Organization as nothing worthy
Gets done without the efficient use of
Time and yet when I see the clouds I do

Remember in the midst of bustle I
Want to embody a cloud's deportment.

To emulate a
cloud's deportment is perhaps
a bit beyond my
present capacity but
I want less frenzied thinking.

At the ending of a downpour as the
Final drops are pelting to the earth and
The sky is clearing and the heat and the
Humidity are palpable the sun

Is beginning to blaze this morning and
I can see the leaves are sparkling with
Drops of water reflecting the sunlight —
But the rising breeze and turning leaves are

Already dispersing the water — and
Then from everywhere I hear the birds sing
Though I don't see them flying and I can
Only suppose that something about the

Quality of this moment has moved them
To a spontaneous commentary.

Only briefly am
I able to absorb all
of the quality
a moment has and perhaps
the birds are more attentive.

Where did my worn out emotions go — the
Unpredictable anger and the sense
Of separation and distance I felt
From people — I remember how worry

Perpetuated itself and how the
Solitary arguments I engaged
Never resolved and how the long walks while
Fantasizing never went anywhere

And I remember the Buddha who said
That we are what we think and all that we
Are arises with our thoughts and with our
Thoughts we make the world and he said speak or

Act with a pure mind and happiness will
Arise because this is the ancient law.

Poised with a
samurai sword
preparing to
strike — clarity
is wonderful.

With the impetus of clarity I
Let my thinking go like a spaniel in
A field of grass and I'm amazed by the
Rambunctious foolishness I see as if

The earth has enflamed the dog and he can't
Jump high enough or run fast enough and
He's torn between the scent here and the smell
There and he's hunting because he wants a

Rabbit to chase and bite — and today I'm
Savoring my simple-minded canine
Energy in love with the enticements
Of the earth and the possibility

That I could get my teeth in a special
Delicacy I'd shake and not let go.

But even in my
reverie I understand
my energy will
dissipate and I'll become
a disconsolate doggie.

A frog has emerged that is the size of
A thumbnail and sometimes it has smooth skin
And sometimes it becomes spiky and it
Is also a chameleon and so

It's called the Punk Rocker Frog — which I think
Is ridiculous because in hundreds
Of years when people read categories
Of creatures they will grasp what the frog can

Do but they won't understand the name when
The species of miscreants with spiky
Orange hair and a dozen earrings and
Leather jackets and predominately

British accents will be forgotten and
Replaced by other forms of rebellion.

We don't use
chariots pyramids
or mummification
anymore — but will
we fly in wing suits?

Some people are crazy enough to wear
A wing suit and stand poised on the tip of
A Mountain and jump — with fabric outstretched
Between their arms and legs and body — and

They fly inches from the rocky edges
Plunging as the eagles do consuming
Miles of air passing inside and outside
Of alpine shadows falling on the slopes

Below — how divine the venture must seem
Flowing within a spectacle of such
Gigantic proportions — discovering
In a human form capability

For soaring with flaming sensations and
A beating heart — and with serenity?

Perhaps a
flying squirrel was
the inspiration
but where on earth did
the courage come from?

Of the things to notice on a sunny
Day by the river I see the swallows
Flitting along the bank and above the
Water encountering no obstacles

Within a wide expanse of air and each
Is turning acrobatically in a
Hunt for bugs they must be swallowing on
The fly and they seem so tiny above

The broad river in the valley of the
Limestone bluffs and so inconsequential
To me they're just a curiosity
That they do hunt together and they do

Return to the river in the spring and
I may open my eyes and see swallows.

As the swallows flit
along the surface of the
river the eagles
linger in lazy circles
up within the sunny sky.

There's not much utility in keeping
Cats beyond the discouragement of mice
But there is the obligation to care
For them within a home I willingly

Do because I find myself calling them
 "Doggies" as a joke they don't understand
Or I'll string together syllables of
Nonsense with dramatic inflection and

They gaze at me with adoration and
I can't get people to do that so when
George my partner in lassitude who would
Sit upon my legs when I sat who chirped

Like a cheerful bird suddenly died I
Grieved the loss of gentle companionship.

Rescued from bitter
cold that froze the tips of his
ears off our new cat
needs adjusting so we say
Henry Henry and Henry.

I borrowed my Dad's glasses one day and
Looked at the garage and saw a spot of
Dried mud so I walked across the grass to
Touch it and it disintegrated from

The wall and that's how we discovered I
Needed glasses and suddenly I could
See the writing on the chalkboard could learn
How to read and suddenly there was an

Explanation for the difficulty
I had in keeping up and I wasn't
"Special" as the teachers said or stupid
As I thought and a physical burden

Was gone and the discouragement I felt
Could dissipate and I began to try.

My brother would fall
on the floor would bubble at
the mouth would shiver
in epileptic fits — but
he became a wrestler.

The leaves are fluttering the branches are
Undulating the foliage is flowing
As drops are pelting from a grey sky and
I hear the pattering of the rain on

The leaves and the accumulation and
Dissipation of wind through the widow —
This is a topsy-turvy morning and
I'm savoring the enveloping cool —

But yesterday the sun was blazing by
Mid morning and the humidity was
Already oppressive so I kept the
Window shut as the air conditioner

Was performing because the pinnacle
Of summer is often quite atrocious.

I accommodate
mosquitoes and horseflies
with a slap — and I
am suspicious of tall grass
anticipating wood ticks.

A crystal glass is weighty in my hand
With the liquid light of the sun and I
Drink and enjoy the water flow in my
Mouth and throat and inside of me with the

Taste of no taste that tastes like nourishment
Like health without anything extra and
Drinking doesn't have to be something I
Do without noticing just as I make

The slightest effort drawing air in my
Nose and appreciate its expansion
Within my lungs and I can sense a wave
Of clarity throughout my body as

The persisting rhythms of life are like
Wind in the leaves and the waves on the sand.

I know the words
needed to find
direction and
then I savor
needing no words.

A wide horizon across the cornfields —
Or a blue expanse beyond the trees — or
The sky visible between the towers
Of a city are beguiling because

Here's the difference between the touchable
And breathable as I measure distance
With my eyes and spot my proximity
Within a ceaselessly transforming sky

But when the sun goes down the dividing
Lines of the horizon vanish and the
Apparent emptiness of the universe
Emerges and distance is threatening —

Reality is layered and there are
Limits to how much I can understand.

My capacity
for logic for measuring
and for ascribing
individual meaning
doesn't touch infinity.

I threw a stone into a placid lake
And waited for the ripples to emerge
As an image of an open mind and
A stray thought that comes unexpectedly

With consequences rippling into
Emotion into behavior and then
Into the reactions of people as
They respond to me as I have prompted

Everything following the one thought that
Arises in an instant seemingly
From nowhere except that I don't have an
Open mind — I have propensities for

Seeing only what I choose to see as
The whole of reality escapes me.

I sit motionless
becoming the placid lake
watching ripples of
thoughts and emotions disperse
pursuing an open mind.

Being in the middle of a lake in
A rowing boat with the water glassy
I'm poised and anticipating any
Moment a jolt of inspiration and

I'm waiting — it's not as if my eyes aren't
Seeing my ears aren't hearing but my mind
Is absent my attention is withdrawn
And I'm struggling to be open — then

Like lightning an idea comes from the
Sky providing direction and then I'm
Able to ply my oars to arch my
Back in a smooth continuous motion —

Knowledge and technique want direction and
I aspire to be a lightning rod.

Does inspiration
come from personality
experience or
the habits of the mind or
does it come from emptiness?

An actor friend described Henry Fonda's
Method for playing a role as he would
Imagine circumstances bearing on
Character and formulate elements

Of personality clumsily as
He incorporated situations
And calculated responses and with
Practice came transformation allowing

The slightest flicker of emotion to
Emanate from a consciousness altered
From his as Henry discovered how to
Lose himself for the portrayal of a

Person caught in a story presenting
A significance worthy of effort.

How often do I
assume a role purposely
manipulating
companions and performing
genuine sincerity?

Some of us are much better with practice
At fashioning a desirable
Persona and added to the gift of
A delectable appearance it's as

Good as money to promenade into
A room and shower sunshine on people
Who are helpless in admiration and
It's a power of brutish beauty that

Flourishes in Hollywood — but there is
A pinnacle in a career after
Which there's nothing more to gain followed
By descent to obscurity as

Other performers take the stage — and can
An aging actor retire with grace?

Adulation and
satisfaction aren't the same —
I want to learn how
to use my energy and
to find a home within me.

The bustle on the boulevards of New
York City and Jimmy Cagney with
His pistols tommy guns and fedoras
Were captured in film with shades of grey and

Jimmy was exciting and glamorous
Impetuous and manipulating
And he turned the elegant women of
The day with his charm but Jimmy's faded

From memory and his élan's overlaid
By generations of stars — and fashion
Has forgotten his masculinity
His desperation and vitality —

He's vanished like the smell of buttery
Popcorn in demolished movie theaters.

Ginger Rogers and
Fred Astaire vivaciously
flamboyantly so
epitomized their era
with swing-time dance and brass bands.

Presiding amidst the nation's heart of
Glamour and gambling in Las Vegas and
Holding sway between flocks of dancers and
Gilding an appetite for decadence

Modest people couldn't afford was the
Rat Pack of the sixties — Frank Dean Sammy
Peter Joey joking singing charming
Taking American culture for a

Ride — but there came a news description of
Dean Martin at eighty relating his
Solitary lunches and regular
Digestion of ribeyes and whiskey with

A failing memory and glassy eyes —
He might have been anyone at that age.

With so much talent
with such opulent venues
and wide exposure
comes exhilaration but
also a tremendous drop.

Clearing the River

Each detail is rough hewn in the photo
Of 1886 from the boards of
The flat bottom boat to the steam engine
And the brimmed hats and the tough working clothes

Of the several lumber jacks with their beards
And mustaches because there's no use for
Delicacy as the river is clogged
With logs in a tangled pile twenty feet

High and the scrawny men in their resting
Postures seem unequal to the task but
It was their business with steel hooked pikes and
Thick cords of rope to clear the river and

Raft the logs downstream as they must have known
How to take advantage of leverage.

Their faces are blurred
but their chosen postures
do communicate
hints of personality —
irreverence and bravado.

Ben Hur 1887 - 1916

It's a day of celebration drawing a
A good crowd to the river and the dock
For a ride on the steamboat Ben Hur and
Perhaps as a part of the festivities

The photo captures the moment and so
I may see everyone facing me on
The three levels a hundred years ago
And each is distinguishable in the

Differences in age in attitude
In fashion in status revealing in
A relaxed and happy presentation
Engagement and eagerness for the day —

So I gaze with curiosity at
An alluring familiarity.

The postures and the
features of the faces in
the vanished moment
present a wide array of
living personality.

I didn't know her but youthful beauty
Communicates the smile appeals and
The camaraderie with her girl friend
Bespeaks a genuineness and so the

Photo of the murdered girl sobers us
As we share it — this moment of sunny
Possibility has been taken from
Her and her child and this living woman

Is bordered in a photo — the man's been
Caught the cause is known she left him but then
Returned and the result is permanent —
Behind closed doors and between lovers how

Could matters have come to this how could she
Have so misjudged him how could he do it?

The brutality
transpiring secretly
within closed doors and
with demeaning words and then
escalating beyond control.

My ancestors were MacDonalds and were
Highlanders in Scotland and because my
Dad came from Australia apparently
Someone in the linage was transported

From England to Australia — this is the
History of my body — but perhaps
I've been a hunter on the African
Savanna a merchant on the Silk Road

Of Asia a noblesse of France a wretch of
The untouchables of India or
An Eskimo and maybe I've been a
Daughter a mother a grandmother and

A scholar a warrior and a thief —
I don't know the history of my births.

My consciousness is
a sojourner of ages
my body provides
genetics but all I have
is what's possible today.

Suppose there's no death and consciousness
Continues and emerges again in a
Mother's embrace gradually seeing
What's me and mine and what's otherwise and

I display abilities and failings
Native to me setting me apart but
Life is a river going on and on
And I encounter impediments and

I innovate and forget and when I'm
Born with new parents the other gender
In different circumstances when I look
In the mirror could I possibly know

Everything I thought I was and whether
I was famous or unremarkable?

Everything in sight —
consciousness and memory
my propensities
my pivotal qualities —
amounts to a soap bubble.

The sinuous dragon flowing in the
Air with fierce eyes leathery wings talons
Appears wild and unpredictable — it's
The stuff of dreams an image of chaos

And a reminder of the potential
For sudden destruction except something
About it has an aspect of purpose
Intelligence as it represents a

Propulsion of ceaseless transformation
A remixing of the elements as
Whatever exists today is bound to
Pass away and assume a different form —

The earth was once a molten lifeless rock
And even distant stars will disappear.

The spirit of the
dragon swallows everything —
the universe has
summoned and determined that
metamorphosis is fact.

Is all of this necessary or just
A little superfluous for the game
Of flirtation as ordinarily
Aren't subtle gestures and hints sufficient

But there's inspiration in the design
In the mixture of the colors with the
Popping of the incandescent green on
The breast the regal crown and the frilly

Fringy sinuousness of the feathers
Made to be displayed as one flicks open
A Japanese folding fan and who could
Look away from the flouncing ensemble?

There isn't an Italian designer
Capable of creating the peacock.

So fashionable
with such superfluity
of beauty — the most
imaginative artist
couldn't dream up the peacock.

I put a dozen peacock feathers in
A marble urn because I love to gaze
At the lovely quills the charming fringes
The blues greens bronzes and purples and I

Think about the bird — how often do they
Preen what do they look like when scampering
And squabbling do they peck at their food
What kind of noises do they make and then

I imagine beautiful women in
Wedding dresses driving the kids to school
And chopping vegetables or arguing
With their husbands and it's ridiculous —

Wouldn't it be a drag to manage such
Superfluous finery everyday?

The panther moves
inconspicuously
surreptitiously
in the night —
yellow eyes watching.

Going to the gym everyday is a
Habit I'm proud of though it's possible
To become narcissistic about my
Progress as I watch my muscles pumping

Iron in the surrounding mirrors and
I've found an obsessive connection in
Pain and satisfaction and I'm likely
To be possessive of the cardio

Machines as I know which run smoothly that
Causes frustration because an older
Fellow often climbs on before me and
He doesn't go as fast I do but

I have to use another machine and
To practice minimizing my ego.

When done I want
a shower and a certain
shower head because
it sprays robustly and
it is the warmest.

Like a basset hound with droopy skin and
Ears baying so mournfully at the moon
And disturbing my sleep I've tossed about
With worry and during the day the hound

Gets his teeth into a rag and won't let
Go no matter how I pull to free myself
From cogitating over offensive
Words and it's useless to ruminate with

Sad eyes with my hound's head between outstretched
Paws on the floor because wherever my
Thoughts go my paws are sure to follow so
I've learned to throw the dog a bone to let

Myself chew joyfully on projects that
Channel enthusiastic energy.

When I'm searching for
the appropriate words and
images to fit
an emerging line of thought
I don't know my tail's wagging.

Who cares about compassion who wants to
Be the chump because it seemed too often
People would see me strolling on the street
And they'd barrel over me in Mack Trucks

Then I'd ruminate and I'd fantasize
About finding a garbage truck biding
Time patiently watching and suddenly
I'd smoosh them leaving an odor behind

But such cogitation seldom led to
Successful smooshings and unhappily
I became the garbage truck trailing an
Odoriferous load behind me so I'm

Trying to surrender my righteousness
Reactive impulses and self-pity.

I don't have to
squish because I
was squashed —
I would rather be
a Maserati.

My writer's group is questioning "why do
You use a ten-syllable line — isn't
It arbitrary and wouldn't it be
Better to let the words flow freely?" so

I thought about why I do what I do
With an eye for justification so
Maybe I am a bit pretentious but
Isn't my way of perceiving the world

Arbitrary — you and I may see the
Same sun but notice differently — and the
Flowing world can only be captured from
A limited point of view — and besides

There's magic in choosing carefully and
Measuring reveals graininess in words.

I appreciate
my idiosyncrasies
and I enjoy
doing what I do —
being eccentric.

For Paul (a Groupie)

They questioned in my writer's group
"Why do you use a ten syllable line?"
"Isn't it arbitrary and wouldn't it be better
To let the words flow freely?"
So, I thought about why I do what I do
With an eye for justification.

So, Maybe I am a bit pretentious, but isn't
My way of perceiving the world arbitrary —
You and I see the same sun but notice differently —
And the flowing world can only be captured
From a limited point of view.

And besides, there's magic in choosing carefully,
And measuring reveals graininess in words.

I appreciate my idiosyncrasies,
And I enjoy doing what I do —
Being eccentric.

I remember arriving at the bay
Taking my helmet off and sitting on
A bench watching the waves coming in from
The ocean enjoying a sunny day

And I thought by playing the romantic
Role of a foreigner in Japan by
Driving a motorbike across Honshu
I could have an adventure and escape

Loneliness but on the bench I knew it
Wasn't true because an aching hole in
Me reminded me I was far from home
And didn't know what to do with myself —

And decades later I've discovered that
Loneliness pushed me to companionship.

It was easier
to leave America and
arrive in Japan
than to endure time and grow
a home in my head and heart.

Berlitz School of Languages

I remember my fellow teachers and
The time we had between lessons in the
Lounge getting to know each other over
Years in five-minute breaks between bouts of

English lessons and each day our rank on
The teacher's board reflected our precious
Seniority and determined who got
Lucky with fluent students and who would

Be mouthing basic verbs again — but the
Room and window overlooking Kyoto
Was a sanctuary where we could be
Ourselves apart from formality and

In the evening if I had a lesson
Off I would always watch Sumo Digest.

Twenty years later
I remember my fellow
teachers with pleasure
with light-hearted memories
but their faces are fading.

There's a bloom of youth in a perfectly
Proportional body in shining skin
In glossy hair approaching pinnacle
Health and I remember running for joy

In appreciation of blossoming
Life knowing that I could never be more
Youthful than now as the mirror informed
Me but then I compared myself with those

More beautiful and handsome than I was
And I noticed their couplings besides
My loneliness and believed the best of
Life was passing me by because I was

Alone because I hadn't learned how to
Overcome the gap between you and me.

The mirror today
shows wrinkles about my eyes
and less hair than I
prefer but I'm not inclined
to cherish appearances.

Do you spend more time thinking about me
Than I do about you because I could
Be writing poetry and you would be
Happier pulling weeds in your garden

But I'm idly sitting and absently
Gazing out the window accomplishing
Nothing but looking studious in an
Offensive manner to you as I should

Be cleaning the aquarium dusting
Or vacuuming and you're doing your best
Not to kick me while I'm pretending to
Be another Shelly Keats or Shakespeare

But how can I concentrate while you are
The epitome of an annoyance?

Somewhere in the sky
there's an eagle flying in
lazy circles as
he's hunting a rabbit but
I'm far too annoyed to see.

Golden Bumble Bees

My bulbous head is a beehive humming
With thoughts and one by one the bees go forth
Voracious for sugary nectar and
Rumbling bumbling and bobbing in summer

But a single bee doesn't amount to
Much it's cumulative exploration
It's a happenstance discovery of
A juicy flower informing the hive

Where the sweetness is and directing the
Buzzing swarm to the garden that hundreds
Of little bee feet may trod on silky
Petals that a multitude of tiny

Bee straws may altogether burrow in
And with accumulating effort suck.

I may be thoughtful
assuming a studious
expression sporting
a furrowed brow but really
I want my juicy honey.

Love isn't what I supposed it was as
It's a fact buried within a busy
Day — when rushing about immersed in my
Habitual way and encountering

Several interruptions preventing me
From getting things done and feeling pressure
Of not having enough time I got a
Call from you about needing to go to

The hospital again which sometimes you
Do because of your diabetes and
With irritation I left my work for
The emergency room again but when

You stopped breathing and nurses gathered to
Save you I crumbled discovering love.

The experience
was not irretrievable
today but it's a
reminder diabetes
gradually progresses.

As the past lingers the present intrudes
And I mistrust memories as I might
Be misremembering but there was the
Night I listened to you coughing during

A trip during an asthma attack when
You forgot your inhaler and I could
Do nothing — and there was the turning of
Personality from the boisterous

And brilliant child to the secretive and
Doubting teenager that puzzles me as
You remain insular and resistant
To my questions as you're leaving home to

Live in Alaska on your own and I
Wonder whether I could have done better.

Because I see you
differently from everyone
because I have my
memories and emotions
and I want you to do well.

There are raindrops in this piece of paper
And the clouds from which the rain came reside
Now within this white form that was once a
Tree that has become a poem because

Without the drops to nurture the tree the
Expression of the tree the paper and
Poem could not be and the minerals
In the soil also live in the paper

Because without minerals soil has no
Potency and the magic of the sun
Rises off the paper to warm your face
As I communicate to you with words —

The loggers the road makers and the mill
Workers have all labored for this poem.

Metamorphosis
is a fact and the magic
is a mystery
and the mystery is deep
though it happens every day.

The Chinese poets who turned their backs on
Imperial politics who left the
Cities for the mountains and the rivers
Who wrote about mountains generating

The clouds and about the tumultuous
Voices of cataracts resonating
Valleys who wrote about solitary
Wanderings about absorbing the shine

Of the moon in a boat while imbibing
Wine seemed to prefer the twilight and the
Moon to the light of day perhaps because
The dark and stars revealed the pathos of

Being that cannot be evaded so
They faced the bare reality with Zen.

Their penetrating
explorations cannot be
surpassed — their insights
cannot be forgotten but
I prefer the morning sun.

I hope you don't mind taking a piece of
My mind as I endeavor to gather
Bits and pieces of stray thoughts and corral
Them and direct them suitably so that

They cohere in a package deal that's not
Altogether disreputable but
Please consider most of the time my mind
Resembles a Mexican jumping bean

Though I've found it's helpful to think about
Something I love — like peaches — and my thoughts
Become of a piece swirling about peaches
As I imagine rubbing the fuzzy

Peach tasting the juicy peach and then I
Become the peach achieving peach of mind.

Peaches do for me
what nothing else can because
when I focus on
peaches my thinking becomes
peaceful — peachy and peachful.

Sanga

We get along fine just as long as the
Subjects dividing us aren't discussed as
We adore the *dharma* and each of us
Has *Buddha* nature — if only we could

Forget ourselves for a moment — but how
To accomplish the forgetting is the
Mystery we share — and it's marvelous
To sit on the edge of perplexity

Together and persevere as we hunt
For the precise posture or attitude
Which somehow defeats our purpose — after
Earnestly practicing I've arrived at

A point where there's nowhere to turn and
No place to stand to grasp enlightenment.

I can't be elsewhere
if I'm sitting right here so
perhaps I'd better
cherish curiosity
practice receptivity.

In late summer on a quiet morning
As the sun is climbing in a clear sky
There's a sense of accumulated growth
Of a conclusion hanging in the air

Because the sun has spent its fire for the
Year and the days are teetering on the
Edge of cooler afternoons and mellow
Light and after experiencing more

Than sixty summers it's natural
To think of the seasons of a life and
A culmination of effort but now
On a bare branch suspended high in the

Air a sparrow perches and it's bobbing
The delicate limb a moment and goes.

The light on the leaves
of the cottonwood is mild
and as they turn in a
breeze I see brown spots and
ragged edges on the leaves.

My mind is adrift in memories of
Childhood salvaging glimpses of events
Like being with my brother and sister
In the car with my mother driving with

Her admonishing against saying "gee"
Because it means "Jesus" and certainly
"Damn" was out and she couldn't say the words
That were worse that we already knew but

She didn't disapprove of "darn" so much
Though saying nothing was much better and
I felt embarrassed and grateful my friends
Weren't there and I revolted deciding

Not to follow such rules because I would not
Be a wussy when she wasn't around.

Sometimes when my kids
break out in crude language I
feel embarrassed that
we didn't talk about how
words can brutalize people.

I bump into myself when I feel the
Propulsion of the word "must" in my mind
As my back and chest tighten as a pang
In my stomach communicates fear and

I get ready to marshal assertion
And I intend to be determined in
Action because from experience I
Know how shame feels when I didn't even

Try — because I've cringed when I've realized
I'll never know what I could have done — but
I'm grateful through many years to be much
Better at seeing opportunities

At summoning effort and in finding
Satisfaction in doing all I could.

After chasing my
share of elusive rabbits
I'm getting better
at seeing ephemeral
clues pointing a direction.

Of Stillwater

There's the illusion of stability
As one day blends into the next and the
Showers of rain and the transforming sky
From cloudy to clear to cloudy are so

Ordinary they're not worth noticing
And the drama of human behavior
Is much more troublesome and the trees have
Been standing here for a long time and the

Leaves are dispersing the temperature
Declining so gradually but as
Autumn progresses and foliage dissolves
I'm able to see the valley again

And realize the river's been moving
Before America was a nation.

How gradually
and irreversibly the
grinding and wearing
progresses and suddenly
I consider the river.

One after another my thoughts go out
Like waves of light radiating from my
Being as if I were a creator
As if anything enfolded within

My consideration was nothing was
Formless until my consciousness gave it
Being and meaning — just as the rising
Sun reveals the trees the valley and the

River from emptiness — I see details
And proximity — I establish the
Context and definitions — I ascribe
Layers of importance — I discover

How love feels and like a child I hunger
To take possession — and capture my love.

The world arises
in the light of sight in the
flame of consciousness —
I create heaven or hell
depending on my thinking.

Something is always going on in my
Head especially when I'm quiet when
I'm weighing and measuring what you do
And how you do it as there a comes day

After a while when you get the urge to
Rearrange the furniture and get rid
Of stuff and buy a new coffee maker
Even though the old one works — as I watch —

And if I tried I couldn't chatter on
As you do about your co-workers and
About the incidents on the job so
I listen just enough to be ready

To answer the question I know you'll ask
That demonstrates that I've been listening.

I could be thinking
about the doings of the
Hottentots or the
Eskimos but in a snap
I'll make affirmative sounds.

This is an unforgiving bicycle
Seat day after day punishing me as
I rub myself raw with effort — but I
Can direct my imagination to

The beauties in spandex on display on
The elliptical machines and treadmills
Or watch people jabber on T.V. and
Listen to music on headphones as I

Assume the same position on the bike
And do the same motion everyday for
An hour as I measure minutes with songs
And I maintain a loose and speedy pace

And my legs are pumping and my torso
Is flexing — I put my mind in a box.

Pain in the right knee
went away and I didn't
change my routine so
I'm guessing I can ignore
the tightness in my left knee.

Mind is a bowl of potentiality
Open to the sky and the universe
Beyond once I've become aware of its
Quality as I have learned to become

Quiet and to let thought settle down so
As to sharpen my sense perceptions
So that I receive messages coming
In waves of sound or light or by a touch

Taste or smell and most suffering results
From the stories I create by way of
Explanation attending a sense of
Self that is overly precious to

Me — but if I practice quietude of
Thought more of the universe resonates.

With thoughts I compose
explanations for the words
and deeds of people
but honestly I confess
I have scant explanation.

This consciousness I have as I do my
Daily activities is easy to
Underestimate because I get snared
While watching T.V. listening to a

Concerned gentleman asking whether I
Have a plan for retirement because
It would be terrible if my living
Outlasted my supply of money — I

Want to taste the piquancy of this
Everlasting moment even when I'm
Teetering between aggravation and
Grace I want the opportunity to

Balance everything I encounter and
Penetrate as deeply as possible.

I want the bare
awareness
underneath
my many threads
of emotion.

Whether you leave your mark by being an
Impediment or obnoxious to me
I have needed you to set my course by
Because nothing's better than frustration

For motivation and whether I'm right
Or wrong I need to muster effort to
Clarify my intentions — and when I
Come to understand being right or wrong

Is a temporary position I
Assume depending on what others do
I hope to channel my energy in a
Manner minimizing self-centeredness

Because the frictions I encounter could
Be the turnings I need for compassion.

Perhaps I'll claim a
truth worthy of following
or maybe I'll see
how I've been mistaken and
deepen my understanding.

In Australia by way of description
Women who wear their hair cut across their
Foreheads are said to have a cheeky fringe
And I've not heard that men having the same

Arrangement qualify for exactly
The same appellation as it seems that
Men ordinarily aren't so worthy
Of special observation as most of

Us are as appealing as an old pair
Of brown shoes because wouldn't you rather
If given a choice rest your eyes upon
The curvaceous and enticing form of

A woman who knows how to posture than
Look at an old boy without any hair?

Yet many of our
male politicians are quite
hairy — perhaps God
grants dispensation for those
who are virtuous and wise.

I consumed a good part of yesterday
Daydreaming about a romance with a
Person I barely know and though there's no
Regret I feel silly about being

Oblivious and infatuated
So this morning while clarity is in
The air I must acknowledge that life now
Isn't everything I dream about but

So what — don't I know what transpires when
Romance wears off and two people are left
With themselves and stripped of illusions and
Didn't I learn how difficult it is

To manage my fountain of emotions
And two together are a tornado?

Curiosity
infatuation pursuit
come naturally
once we've acquired a taste
for romance — God save us all.

Each morning I sequester myself in
A steel machine and by pressing down with
My foot I can go as fast as I want
And I can go anywhere I want by

Turning a wheel with my hands and there are
Roads to the Pacific or Atlantic
Or I could go to Mexico but I
Tend to stay in Stillwater and mostly

I follow a predictable route and
A daily schedule as if I were a
Mouse in a maze and though I seem as free
As birds are I don't want to go elsewhere

Because wherever I go my habits go
Too and if I leave my friends stay home.

I drive in summer
autumn winter and spring and
every season I'm
noticing something different
that I've never seen before.

That Tree

The photographer returned to an Ash
Tree on the rise of a curvaceous plain
In North Dakota and fixing the tree
Within the grass a wide horizon and

The sky he captured the sight over years
And in spring the grass is green in summer
Yellow in autumn brown and on a day
In winter the grass and the sky are white —

And then the grass and the tree are white but
The sky has turned blue — and through the seasons
Clouds are clustered or dissipated but
One evening a setting sun shone on a

Canopy of clouds producing tinges
Of yellow gold orange red and purple.

From the emptiness
of a horizontal plain
in North Dakota
the colors of the rainbow
are passing through.

Not only the plunge in temperature
And having to scrape a frosting from my
Windshield with the dawn for the first time — but
Also the prominence of red orange

And yellow leaves on the trees I pass — and
The swirls on the streets of the leaves in the
Gusts of the wind — and also the fact that
The sun is lacking the fire of summer —

All these things point to the necessity
Of taking cover and bundling up
For a coming winter again as the
Wheel of the seasons is turning once more —

The trees emulate the flowers and bloom
And then they stand twiggy in the winter.

It's ironic how
the autumn leaves resemble
holiday colors
before dissipating and
I do want to celebrate.

The Stonehenge

When driving along a street and seeing
The morning sun and a crescent moon a
Thought arose of the stone masters who have
Vanished from the earth and all that remains

Are their meticulous monuments as
Evidence of their piercing insight that
They followed the stars and moon they channeled
The rising sun — and the capacity

Of their bodies the ingenuity
Of their mastery is evident in
The cutting of and the assembly of
The gargantuan stones — but no one knows

Much about them and the constellations
Have moved on leaving the stones out of tune.

Perhaps I was a
carver of the faces on
Easter Island and
set them up under the stars
but I'm not remembering.

A rascal put a
snail shell in a
tuba —
rumble has rattle
curlicue in curves.

— *Tekkan*

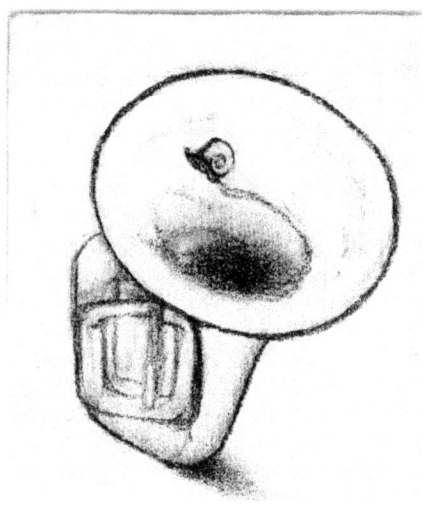

www.ingramcontent.com/pod-product-compliance
Lightning Source LLC
Chambersburg PA
CBHW052104070526
44584CB00017B/2324